ALL ABOARD!

STEAM-POWERED TRAINS

Phillip Ryan

PowerKiDS press™

New York

Published in 2011 by The Rosen Publishing Group, Inc.
29 East 21st Street, New York, NY 10010

First Edition

Editor: Joanne Randolph
Book Design: Ashley Burrell
Photo Researcher: Jessica Gerweck

Photo Credits: Cover © www.iStockphoto.com/Dave Wetzel; p. 5 © Russ Bishop/age fotostock; pp. 6–7, 14–15 Shutterstock.com; p. 9 John Kelly/Getty Images; p. 10–11 © José Fuste Raga/age fotostock; p. 13 © Claver Carroll/age fotostock; p. 17 © Gavin Hellier/age fotostock; p. 18–19 © Phillip Wallick/age fotostock; p. 21 © Sylvain Grandadam/age fotostock; p. 22–23 Michael Cogliantry/Getty Images.

Library of Congress Cataloging-in-Publication Data
Ryan, Phillip.
  Steam-powered trains / Phillip Ryan. — 1st ed.
     p. cm. — (All aboard!)
  Includes index.
  ISBN 978-1-4488-0640-9 (library binding) — ISBN 978-1-4488-1221-9 (pbk.) —
ISBN 978-1-4488-1222-6 (6-pack)
  1. Steam locomotives—Juvenile literature. 2. Railroads—Juvenile literature. I. Title.
  TJ605.5.R93 2011
  625.26′1—dc22
                          2009052022

Manufactured in the United States of America

CPSIA Compliance Information: Batch #WS10PK: For Further Information contact Rosen Publishing, New York, New York at 1-800-237-9932

CONTENTS

Have you ever seen a steam-powered, or steam, train? Trains ride on **tracks**.

Steam trains have jobs to do. This steam train carries goods.

6

This steam train carries people. It picks them up at a **station**.

Steam trains carry goods and people all over. This train goes over a bridge.

This steam train rolls through hills. The tracks twist and bend to follow the land.

The first car in a steam train is called the **engine**.

14

Coal can be used to give the engine power. Here you can see the coal for this engine.

The engine has a **smokestack**. Big clouds of smoke come out of it.

18

Steam trains run in all kinds of weather. This train is ready to do its job on a snowy day.

If you could ride a steam train, where would you want to go?

WORDS TO KNOW

engine   smokestack

station   tracks

INDEX

WEB SITES

Due to the changing nature of Internet links, PowerKids Press has developed an online list of Web sites related to the subject of this book. This site is updated regularly. Please use this link to access the list:
www.powerkidslinks.com/allabrd/st/